The A - Z of Family Life:

Karlene Rickard

Published by
Filament Publishing Ltd
16, Croydon Road, Beddington, Croydon
Surrey CR0 4PA
www.filamentpublishing.com
+44(0)20 8688 2598

©2019 Karlene Rickard

ISBN 978-1-912635-92-4

The right of Karlene Rickard to be identified as the author of this work has been asserted by her in accordance with the Designs and Copyrights Act 1988 Section 77

All rights reserved
No portion of this work may be copied in any way without the prior written permission of the publishers

Printed by IngramSpark

The A - Z of Family Life: Dedication

To my son, Pianki and his family. Archana, my daughter-in-law and Shay my grandson. Use this book as an effective parenting tool in your role as parents, teacher and mentor.

Also to Tracey Ann Alecia Warner, my spiritual daughter, confidante and friend. You have inspired, motivated and challenged me, without ceasing, into my God given destiny.

Acknowledgements

Firstly I would like to acknowledge God for sustaining me through MS, brain injury and other serious health concerns. I thank God for inspiring me to record the twenty sic parenting tools recorded in this book. These invaluable tools are building blocks for healthy families, resulting in healthy communities and ultimately culminating in healthy nations.

Finally I would like to acknowledge my Pastor and friend Christopher Hutchinson who demonstrated his confidence in me, by appointing me as the first Parenting Director in the New Testament Church of God. I also thank Christopher for painstakingly editing the manuscript for this book.

Contents

	Dedication	3
	Acknowledgements	4
	Preface by Jacqueline Thompson	6
	Introduction	7
A	Appreciation	8
B	Beliefs	10
C	Communication	12
D	Diet	14
E	Emotional Intelligence	16
F	Financial Literacy	18
G	Goal	20
H	Holidays	22
I	Integrity	14
J	Justice	26
K	Keys for a Successful Life	28
L	Love	30
M	Modelling	32
N	Nurture	34
O	Opportunity	36
P	Physical Exercise	38
Q	Quality Time	40
R	Responsibility	42
S	Sexuality	44
T	Technology	46
U	Unity	48
V	Values	50
W	Wisdom	52
X	Relax and Let Go	54
Y	Y as in Boundary	56
Z	Zero Tolerance for Abuse	58
	About the author - Mary Cowley OBE	61

Preface

Every individual has a family. This can be by birth, formal adoption or mutual adoption. However we come by our families the life within them is fundamental to us achieving, or not, self-actualisation.
Family is important to society.

Families are made up of adults and children who are related to each other either by blood or through marriage. Healthy families are fundamental to contributing to and creating a healthy and productive society.

Families are micro ecosystems where communication, education, values and love are central to the overall development of all within the family structure. At the beginning of the relationship between parents and their children, the focus is on providing for and raising their children. Sometimes this can be to the detriment of the personal growth and development of the parents.

In this book Karlene guides you through the key points of family life and stresses the importance of families growing together and individually. Karlene shines a spotlight on what family life is and consciously unpicks what makes families function, within the home and outside of it. Karlene celebrates families, their influence and all they bring to society.

Jacqueline Thompson

Introduction

The A to Z of Family Life is the second publication on the important subject of parenting. It builds of the popular and successful 'A to Z of Parenting' and also covers effective strategies for parenting.

In the A to Z of Family Life, I have continued my alphabetic format. This approach provides a fun and interesting way of communicating the information as well as aiding in the retention of the material. This book integrates time tested principles for effective parenting with fresh and insightful perspectives. ...

In this work, readers will have a veritable tool kit of ideas to address many of the challenges with engaging our children and young people.

I am grateful to those individual who have assisted in producing this second instalment: to the contributors who have added their own ideas and perspectives, the proof readers who have painstakingly reviewed the material, to the publishers for their encouragement and patience and to family members for their eternal support.

Karlene Rickard

Appreciation

Family is the building block to our community; community is the building block to our nation and our nation to our world

The greatest desire of all persons is to have the attention and appreciation of their family and friends. Therefore, it is important that family members and friends should pay attention to and interact with each other and have fun. It is wonderful to observe something new about each other every day and to praise our children for positive behaviour, attitudes, effort or achievement. Most importantly, we must praise family members for just being who they are. Then we will be praising each other more often.

Parents can ignore some of the less severe, unwanted behaviours. Eventually they will stop. Of course, if our children are putting themselves, others or properties at risk, we need to deal with the situation immediately.

What to Do

i. Praise each other Daily
ii. Move close to the person.
iii. Call the person by name.
iv. Look pleased to be with that person.
v. Say to the person exactly what the praise is about. With children, say what you have heard them say or have observed them doing and demonstrate your appreciation through praise. Be specific, for example "I really like the way you styled your hair."
vi. Say to each other exactly how you feel about them.
vii. Family members should show each other physical affection; you could give a hug or just a gentle touch.
viii. Parents, you can give new responsibilities to encourage the continued development of the observed qualities, for example, letting your child style your hair.
ix. Family members, openly praise each other in the presence of other members of the family or friends.

Beliefs

There are many ways of regarding human spirituality. For some people, spirituality is closely associated with a religious belief, for others it is not.

Some regard spirituality as the ultimate state of being to which they can aspire as humans. For others, it has to do with acknowledging the greatness of nature and the wonders of the world. A spiritually focused person can be said to be someone who stands in awe of what is not understood. Some people associate spirituality with something they call the supernatural.

Spiritual development plays a critical part in our becoming balanced and stable individuals. Although our spiritual dimension is not measurable, it is an essential part of our lives. Our spiritual well-being is associated with our beliefs, therefore, we need to share our spirituality, beliefs and faith with others and our children when they are young so that they can develop their own beliefs. When they become teenagers, and if negative peer pressure starts to impact on their lives, they will be in a much better position to resist if their spiritual beliefs are strong. If their beliefs and spiritual foundation is weak they are likely to be more easily influenced by others and anything.

What to Do

i. Ensure that everyone in the family is aware of the family belief

ii. Talk to your child about your beliefs. For example, "I believe that we were created by God and he has made all of us unique and special with a specific purpose to be fulfilled in our lives".

iii. Parents must train their children and teach them how to be constant in their belief through praying together, devotion, sharing their salvation experience if they believe in it.

iv. Talk about the three dimensional make-up of human beings: body, soul, spirit and how they work together to create harmony.

v. Have a time of reflection and sharing of testimonies and some of the spiritual or supernatural experiences.

vi. Everyone should feel free and confident to share some of the fears and challenges they have faced and how they were able to overcome them.

vii. Parents should demonstrate ways in which their beliefs are practiced, such as giving to charity, meditating, or modelling how they pray.

Communication

We need to be able to communicate effectively in order to live a balanced and healthy life. This can be verbal or non-verbal.

Children need to become aware that everyone, including themselves, has the right to be heard and respected therefore we have to be sensitive and caring when communicating, whilst ensuring that our own views are made clear.
We can put communication styles into three groups:

Aggressive Communication
This is where our main concern is that our own thoughts, ideas, and opinions are heard and accepted. Views are also expressed in a hostile and insensitive manner without regard for other person's opinions and feelings.

Passive Communication
This is where we fail to express our true thoughts and feelings, or express them without conviction. We give away our rights to others and allow them to dismiss our suggestions and opinions.

Assertive Communication
This is where our main concern is that our own thoughts, ideas, opinions, as well as those of the person we are communicating with, are expressed openly and honestly.

What to Do

i. The family should discuss the three styles of communicating. You could role-play the different styles to give a clear feel of what they are like.

ii. Discuss in the family about:
   a. the feelings that result when we experience the different communication styles and ask your family members to share occasions when they may have experienced the different styles.
   b. the communication styles they have experienced in their day to day life and
   c. what is likely to happen when different communication styles are used.

iii. Family members should practice the different kinds of communication styles. Emphasise that the best way to communicate is when one is being assertive, listening carefully and putting one's point of view forward in a strong, but sensitive manner such as: "I can see why you might be anxious about this given what happened before. However, this situation is not the same. I have learned from the previous experience and this will help me to grow and develop."

iv. Family members should identify times when negative communication has taken place, either in the home, at school, in the work environment or at church. Talk about what may have caused them to be negative and look at what could have been done to make the communication more effective.

Diet

To stay youthful and healthy we need to pay close attention to our diets. Nutrition greatly affects the state of our minds and bodies. We are what we eat.

How well we parent is likely to be greatly affected by the state of our health.

We become what we eat. It is important that we are fed a tasty, enjoyable, healthy and balanced diet. In a balanced diet the meal should include foods from the basic food groups. The body must be fed but not just by filling the stomach with anything. The kinds of food we eat are very important.

Young children need a lot of protein to develop as well as vitamins and minerals for protection against diseases. More active individuals need extra carbohydrate for energy.

In addition, they need to take some form of regular exercise in order to build strength, stamina and flexibility. This might be an aerobics class, running, basketball or a dance class.

Consuming sufficient water is critical to our general health since our bodies are over 70% water. Many schools now encourage pupils to carry a bottle of water to class and to drink it when they are thirsty. This greatly aids concentration.

What to Do

Feed your child on a daily basis from the basic food groups. These are as follows:

Proteins

Protein is required to build and repair all tissues, produce antibodies, fight infection, supply energy and form the basis for blood and hormones. Some healthy sources of protein are Soya milk, yogurt, cheese, poultry, fish, beans, pulses, tofu and nuts.

Carbohydrates

Carbohydrates are required to supply energy and to help the body to use other nutrients. Some good sources of carbohydrate are bread, cereal, rice, sweet potatoes and yam.

Fats, Oils

Fats and oils supply food energy. Essential fatty acids provide for healthy skin and protect delicate organs. Some good sources are olive oil, corn oil, hemp oil, oily fish and avocados.

Vitamins and minerals

Vitamins and mineral keep the skin and nervous system healthy, help convert sugars and starchy foods to energy and heat, help the body to resist diseases, provide for healing as well as absorption of calcium to make bones.

Healthy sources of vitamins include guavas, mangoes, peas, carrots, leafy vegetables, spinach, cabbage, bananas, apples and melon. Healthy sources of minerals include turnips, parsley, green bananas, kelp and spirulina (types of algae or fibre).

Fibre helps to keep the bowels working regularly and provides us with some nutrients. Healthy sources of fibre include the following: wholegrain rice, beans, pulses, dates, figs, prunes, lentils, cabbage, kale and oats.

Emotional Intelligence

If we don't acknowledge our emotions, especially anger and grief, our unresolved emotions may cause us to behave irresponsibly or have an adverse effect on our health. For example, suppressed grief has been found to have a strong link to cancer. I once counselled a man who suffered from a stroke because his family discouraged him from crying over the death of his father. At our opening session, after we discussed this, he wept openly, which startled me because I had never heard a grown man weep with such intensity before.

It is important to help our children to recognise their emotions and to soar like eagles by managing their emotional world. It is very important that we allow our children to feel what they are feeling and to express their feelings in some way. In our society, anger is often discouraged in girls and sadness is discouraged in boys. This is not helpful. An emotional vocabulary is as important as an academic one.

It is okay to be angry or sad. It is how these emotions are managed that is more important. Our emotions are a choice and should never be allowed to rule us. Hurting others when we are hurt resolves nothing. It makes matters worse.

Having feelings is part of our humanity, and our feelings need to be honoured. How we express our emotions will be influenced by our individuality and our cultural heritage.

What to Do

i. Make it a habit to talk openly about the whole range of your feelings within the family. For example, let it show when you are excited and talk about your excitement.
ii. Manage angry feelings even if it is challenging. When we are angry it is important to say so and explain why. By stating clearly that we are angry, we are taking ownership of our feelings and modelling appropriate anger management.
iii. When feeling overwhelmed, take a deep breath and count to ten inside.
iv. Tell your family member you are angry about their behaviour or attitude and you will discuss it later.
v. Be careful to separate your feelings about the behaviour from your feelings about the person.
vi. When you are ready, deal with what has happened in a fair way.
vii Be prepared to listen to the other person's point of view. This will help build good relationship by demonstrating that the individual is worthy of respect (i.e. worth listening to). It will also develop that person's confidence to speak frankly.

Financial Literacy

Financial literacy is the ability to make informed judgement concerning money matters and take effective actions with respect to current and future finance.

This should start in the home. It is very easy to become a great consumer instead of investing and developing business in our highly materialistic culture. As parents, we need to be clear about how we manage our finances and what we model to our children. Without financial planning both long and short-term spending will be irrational, families will become predominantly consumers which will lead to impoverishment.

Some of us allow our money to manage us rather than the other way around.

The whole family needs to know how to spend, save and invest money. Children need to be educated about effective money management so that in later life they will become financially independent.

It is important to start teaching our children about money from an early age.

What to Do

i. Ensure all your expenditure is covered and you know your disposable income.
ii. Establish short, medium and long-term plans for family finance. Set goals.
iii. Invest wisely
iv. Help the children to become financially literate by encouraging them to save and use their own money for a range of purposes.
v. Show the child how to invest money in a savings account, for example, and see it grow.
vi. Discuss different ways of saving and work out the most effective ways suitable to them.
vii. Give the children pocket money and help them to budget.
viii. Discuss the importance of making quality purchases by explaining how to compare the price, type and quality of different items.
ix. The family should play cards and educational board games together, for example, Scrabble and Monopoly in order to develop their monetary vocabulary, strategic playing and their skills in handling money.
x. Family should if possible give to charity and to pay their dues or tithes (one tenth of one's income paid to charity or the church) and offering.

Goal Setting

Goal setting (also goal setting theory) involves the development of an action plan designed to motivate and guide a person or group toward a goal. Goal setting can be guided by goal-setting criteria (or rules) such as SMART – Specific, Measurable, Attainable, Real & Reliable, Time-bound criteria. ,

Goal setting is a major component of personal-development and management literature. The theory is a powerful process for thinking about your ideal future, and for motivating yourself to turn your vision of this future into reality. The process of setting goals helps you choose where you want to go in life. By knowing precisely what you want to achieve it provides focus, shapes our dreams, gives us the ability to hone in on the exact actions we need to perform to achieve everything we desire in life.

Goals are great because they cause us to stretch and grow in ways that we never have before. Life is designed in such a way that we look long-term and live short-term. We dream for the future and live in the present. Unfortunately, the present can produce many difficult obstacles, but setting goals provides long-term vision in our lives. We all need powerful, long-range goals to help us get past those short-term obstacles.

What to Do

i. Critically assess the level of satisfaction. Key aspects to learn and remember when studying and writing our goals the only way we can reasonably decide what we want in the future and how we'll get there is to know where we are right now and what our current level of satisfaction is.
   a. Take some time to think through and write down your current situation
   b. Look at your achievements and your pursuit of the vision you have for life this shows you where you are so you can determine where you need to go.
   c. Take some time to reflect, then set some goals in relation to your vision or dream. Be SMART
   d. Think about what is meaningful to you
   e. Identify your best possible self

ii. Prioritize these areas:
   a. Start narrowing down.
   b. Determine who will be involved
   c. Set regular time to evaluate and reflect. See where you are and write it down so that as the months progress you can see just how much ground you are gaining

Holidays

Family holidays should be one of the highlights of the year, it should be planned carefully. Every family should plan for family holidays and they should consider the needs of every member of the family. It should be considered an opportunity to resolve issues, strengthen and reinforce attachment between the members of the family by talking to each other, eating, playing and doing things together.

If the basics of a family holiday are right, you'll return with good and fond memories. These days, everyone seems so busy that it can be hard to find time for family activities so it's important to make time. It is an indicator of how important family ties are regarded. They are the people who know everything about us and accept us anyway.

What to Do

i. Plan holiday as a family, have a family meeting and let everyone share what they would like as a family.

ii. Ensure that the budget can accommodate the needs of every member in the family, then look at a number of options that can fulfil the desire of everyone.

iii. Have another meeting and discuss with family, once decided carry out the decisions.

iv. In cases where the family cannot afford to spend on a holiday away from home they could have an imaginary holiday abroad while still at home with members of the family doing role play.

Integrity

Integrity is having the quality of high moral principles, being reliable and trustworthy; you can be trusted to do the right thing in words and deed. Therefore not saying one thing and doing another. Samuel Johnson noted that, "Integrity without knowledge is weak and useless, and knowledge without integrity is dangerous and dreadful."

People who enrich or elevate themselves at the expense of others are without integrity. Integrity's overriding quality is wholeness. In fact, the word integrity is derived from the same root word as integer, meaning whole. In other words, no discrepancy exists between one's public life and one's private life. People of integrity have nothing to hide and nothing to fear. Integrity embodies the sum total of our being and our actions. Integrity is not something we have, but something we are.

Integrity is a God-like life of consistency and sincerity with no deception or pretence. According to the Bible God is unchangeable: the same yesterday, today, and forever. He is faithful, trustworthy, true, and loyal. He can be counted on. His Word is everlasting.

When everything is stripped away, our name, reputation, and character are all we have. For the sake of our churches, our families, and our very lives, a life of integrity is required.

What to Do

i. Walk in integrity, do not ignore the feelings of others.

ii. Do not ignore your own feelings either.

iii. Parents, encourage your children to do a motive check. If it's more about you than it is about them, get on your knees and confess it. This is a selfish motivation.

iv. Become the person you want your child to become.

v. As you work on your children's character, enlist a friend, or see a counsellor.

vi. Educate yourself. Make it a personal priority. The healthier you get, the better chance your children have of seeing what life can really be

Justice

Justice means to describe someone or something accurately, it is being fair, that is everyone is being treated the same. It is the principle of moral rightness and decency that is up holding of what is right, conformity to truth, fact, or sound reasoning.

Every member of the family is entitled to respect and to be treated justly.

In the family it is so important to ensure that each developmental stage in our children's lives is acknowledged, worked through appropriately and celebrated. This is known as the rite of passage.

What to Do

i. Communicate and behave appropriately with each member of the family.

ii. In setting rules the family should ensure that the rules are fair.

iii. With regard to young children the family should ensure that safety and non-negotiable issues are enforced with age-appropriate explanations.

iv. Each member of the family should be treated according to their age and position of responsibility.

v. With a younger child, be sure to constantly reinforce what you expect and need them to do.

Keys for a successful life

Whether it is preparing for exams, learning a skill, developing healthy and rewarding relationships, or having successful careers there are definite ways to succeed.

Successful people are not quitters. In being successful talent, luck, and opportunity can play a part, but if you follow these basic principles outlined in What To Do you will definitely succeed.

What To Do

i. Have a Plan. This includes having clearly defined goals and the means to assess whether you've attained your goals. Research demonstrates that goal setting works.

ii. Study and learn, develop social competence, or social intelligence, to get ahead.

iii. Learn From Failures. All too often, we focus on the strategies that allow us to succeed. Yet, research tells us that we learn more from studying our failures than we do from success.

iv. Do an "after action review" (to borrow a term from military training), whereby you analyze what happened.

v. Figure out why and how things went wrong and fix them in order to succeed the next time. Renowned leaders of nations and companies will often mention that it was learning from failures that led to their ultimate success.

vi. Celebrate Small achievements. Motivational psychologists know that large accomplishments are easier to achieve if they are broken down into smaller units, and if you reward yourself at each step of the way.

vii. Be persistent. Many successful entrepreneurs and politicians failed many times, and had major setbacks, before they ultimately succeeded. Don't give up and keep working toward that goal.

Love

Love is a strong emotion which connects people together. It is made stronger by accepting one self, being honest and open. Three qualities of love are trust, respect and honesty.

Bible definition of Love

The definition of the three Greek words used to describe the various types of love are the following: Eros is sexual or romantic in nature, Phileo is a brotherly affection toward someone we really like, Agape, which is the deepest love, means doing good things for another person.

What to Do

i. Be honest about your feelings and those of other family members

ii. Smile at family members when they walk in the room, simply because you're happy to see them.

iii. Catch your child (and partner) doing something good and praise them in public for it.

iv. Be sure and share as many family meals together as possible throughout the week

v. Don't compare anyone to another person as everyone is a unique individual and needs to know that you support him or her for who he or she is.

vi. Express love openly and regularly.

vii. Be interested in each other's endeavours and achievements.

viii. Learn to become a better listener especially when family members want to share their feelings.

ix. Schedule regular dates with each of your children and partner throughout the month.

x. Each member of the family should be kind to self. Showing your family that you value taking care of yourself is extremely important in sending a message of how valuable self-love is for the better good of the rest of the family.

Modelling

Modelling is the first and most effective mode of teaching. If our children shout and then we bellow, 'Speak quietly I am not deaf' we are modelling that it is fine to shout. We may insist that they do their homework in a quiet room because a good education is important, yet the chances are, they will see us watching the television more often than they see us reading.

Parents, we often get mad at our teenager for not washing up the plates, but when they were growing up, they were allowed to sit and watch television whilst we washed up. Parents have shown them it is okay to let others do all the household chores.

In small thoughtless ways parents often treat their own parents and others unkindly yet get upset if their children are disrespectful to them.

Parents need to consistently speak quietly to their children in order to model right communication. When their children shout, parent need to remain calm and refuse to respond to their shouting. Life is more caught than taught, so we need to be very careful about what we are modelling.

What to do

i. Be as conscious about the things you do as the things you say. It is what you do that will most influence your child's behaviour and attitude.

ii. Model the calm manner in which you would like your child to communicate with you.

iii. Give special time to each child if you have more than one.

iv. Give special time for self and each other. This will demonstrate that everyone is loved and respected. If father spends special time with his daughter, she will develop a sense of what to expect from a partner when she is of age.

v. Show lots of affection to family members daily and the young children will do likewise.

vi. Always say: "please" and "thank you" and give explanations for social rules and insist on them from your children. They will develop good social skills as a result.

vii. Boys need to observe their fathers contributing to the running of the household in a range of ways and not just seeing them carrying out DIY tasks.

viii. Boys and girls should be expected and be encouraged to do housework, cooking and gardening and to develop a range of survival life skills to be able to live independently.

ix. There are certain behaviours and attitudes that you can develop in your child by introducing them to books and films that portray good role models. For example, the book Gifted Hands by Dr Ben Carson models someone overcoming mental and social barriers to become a great pioneer within the medical field (He was the first doctor to separate Siamese twins who are still alive today).

Nurture

Nurture is the process of nourishing and promoting the development of a child or of oneself, that is, . spirit, soul and body. It includes raising and caring for an infant human being. This involves learning, feeding and supporting.

Biology states that it is the sum of environmental influences and conditions acting on an organism, especially in contrast to heredity. Social science states that it is the fostering or overseeing of the development of something. Nurturing includes knowledge, to educate, to feed, to promote and sustain the growth and development of hopes; cultivating tolerance; fostering friendly relationships.

In the family there are two parts firstly parents self-care is something they do child-free, to care for themselves and the second part is the parents' care for the children. Self-care is essential not only to enable the parents to remain patient, but also to enable them to experience the joy and delight that is present in every day challenges with your family, even the tough ones (days and children). Children love our joyful presence. They respond by becoming happier and more cooperative. No matter what our child does, it's our response that determines the weather in our home. When we forget to give ourselves the attention we need we become a resentful, negative and impatient parent. Husbands and wives should nurture their marital relationship.

What to Do

i. Promote self-care. Self-care can be simply breathing normally while you are sitting with a screaming child or in the midst of a chaotic situation.

ii. Have a cup of tea while you read your child a book.

iii. Go out to dance and various classes on your own,

iv. Ensure there is a balanced and appropriate diet for every member of the family

v. Be more patient.

vi. Relax. If you're finding yourself frequently resentful, or exhausted, if your mind chatter often includes negative thoughts about your family have family meetings and take pampering time e.g massage sauna.

vii. Make it a habit to tune into yourself as often as possible throughout your day. Just take a deep breath and let it flood your body with well-being. Breathe in calm, breathe out stress, your breath helps you be more present with yourself, an essential form of "attention" that we all need.

viii. Celebrate relations. It is a time for relatives living in different places to come together, share a special meal, and celebrate.

Opportunity

Opportunity means a chance to grow, change, learn new things and to do things better than before – as individuals and team. It also means exploring earlier unknown territories to identify potential improvement and growth areas for your brand and business.

Opportunities, however, mean little if you don't have the time to identify the most attractive possibilities at hand, evaluate your options, make choices necessary to place your preference and then develop those opportunities into something that makes a real difference to your world. These are some quotes of opportunity from recognised people:

- "A pessimist sees the difficulty in every opportunity; an optimist sees the opportunity in every difficulty." (Winston Churchill)

- "Opportunity is missed by most people because it is dressed in overalls and looks like work." (Thomas A. Edison)

- "Ability is nothing without opportunity." (Napoleon Bonaparte)

- "Failure is simply the opportunity to begin again, this time more intelligently." (Henry Ford)

- "You never let a serious crisis go to waste. And what I mean by that it's an opportunity to do things you think you could not do before." (Rahm Emanuel)

What to Do

i. Seize every opportunity. "One secret of success in life is for a man to be ready for his opportunity when it comes" (Benjamin Disraeli)

ii. Act in a timely manner. The two worst strategic mistakes to make are acting prematurely and letting an opportunity slip

iii. Create opportunities in the family to grow and develop

Physical Exercise

Exercise is physical activity that is planned, structured, and repetitive for the purpose of conditioning any part of the body. Exercise is used to improve health and maintain fitness. It is performed for various reasons, including increasing growth and development, preventing aging, strengthening muscles and the cardiovascular system, honing athletic skills, weight loss or maintenance, and also enjoyment.

Frequent and regular physical exercise boosts the immune system, helps prevent certain "diseases of affluence" such as coronary heart disease, type 2 diabetes, and obesity. It may also help prevent stress and depression, increase quality of sleep, help promote or maintain positive self-esteem, improve mental health, maintain steady digestion and treat constipation and gas, regulate fertility health, and augment an individual's sex appeal or body image. Childhood obesity is a growing global concern due to lack of physical exercise.

Apart from the health advantages, benefits may include different social rewards for staying active while enjoying the environment of one's culture. Individuals have chosen to exercise publicly outdoors where they can congregate in groups, socialize, and appreciate life. In the United States, a Surgeon General's 1996 report stated that every adult should participate in moderate exercise, such as walking, swimming, and household tasks, for a minimum of 30 minutes daily.

What to Do

i. Have your family set effective physical fitness goals that are specific, achievable that everyone can achieve together, stick with it until physical activity becomes a part of the family's routine.

ii. Set a goal like walking for 30 minutes a day, three times a week.

iii. Issue a family challenge to see who can be the first to achieve a particular task within a given time.

iv. Take regular walks for 10 minutes every morning

v. Schedule aerobics together for 15 to 30 minutes every day.

vi. Do something that gets your heart pumping: biking, running, playing , fast walking, skating, etc.

vii. To stay motivated, sign up for a fun run, a charity bike ride, or the school track and field programme.

Quality Time

The quantity and quality of the time we spend with our family members are both important. However, it is ultimately the quality of time that matters more. Limited quality time is much more effective than a lot of time spent together without any positive interaction.

We need to make our family members know that they are special by giving them both quantity and quality time. We can ask ourselves the following questions when thinking about quality time.

How often do we have special time with each other, doing activities such as walking for pleasure, reading and playing together?
Is that quality time negotiated and is it really time?

It is good to get into a routine whereby you have protected, regular time together. If you are unable to keep to the arranged time, remember to apologise, explain and reschedule. Quality time will provide the platform to develop a positive and healthy relationship.

What to Do

i. Secure a regular and a consistent time for the family when everyone can give full attention and can simply enjoy being together. In these spaces it is important that you can just listen to what each has to say, if anyone wants to talk ,without being critical or forcing solutions on others.

ii. Observe moments of silence. Quality time does not have to be full of speaking and doing. Moments of silence by the river bank or in a hammock as you both read are perfectly valid.

iii. Treasure the memories. How much time each child needs is a very individual matter but generally speaking, under fours need a minimum of about 15 minutes each day and for older children, at least an hour a week. Teenagers need quality time too! Even in adulthood, quality time with our parents is still important and can provide many treasured memories.

iv. Be positive. During quality time together, give each other the opportunity to relax, have fun together and allow yourself to be a little vulnerable. Quality time is most certainly not the time to be reprimanding each other about any behaviour that is disapproved of.

v. Encourage each one to share his or her interests, activities, favourite foods and experiences. Use as many opportunities as possible to get to know each other.

vi. Do not judge. Spouses in particular should have quality time together listening to each other.

Responsibility

It is the right of our children to be given responsibilities. The United Nations convention states that, "it is a child's right to participate in society".

No child is too young to be given responsibility. What is critical is that the responsibility is age appropriate. When we do not give our children appropriate responsibilities, we rob them of opportunities to become creative, inventive and self-reliant.

Education is not just about going to school and learning how to read and write. A rounded education will include the development of a sense of responsibility for oneself and towards others. A child needs to know from a young age how to take responsibility for themselves and their actions and the home is the place to teach such principles. For example, looking after younger siblings is one way our children can learn to be responsible for others.

Even before children are brought into existence the adult members of the family must understand their responsibilities to themselves and toward others. Fathers and potential fathers must understand that they have primary responsibility as the men of the family to provide for the well-being of all the family and to provide leadership without trampling the rights of other members of the family.

This is a role which calls for great courage and spiritual as well as physical strength. It also calls for great sensitivity.

The women in the family usually deal with the nurturing role for which they are generally well fitted.

Coordination, planning, strategic thinking, time management and cooperation are some of the essential skills that are developed when family members have responsibilities.

What to Do

i. Give your children age appropriate responsibilities. For example, give little jobs around the house to the younger ones, such as tidying up shoes, folding socks etc. with supervision as necessary.

ii Older children should be given duties according to their abilities

Sexuality

Sexuality refer to a person's gender identity, the core sense that we are female or male. It includes how we feel about our bodies. We call that "body" image. A person with poor body image may not think they deserve a good partner, and so they may be willing to settle for someone who will not respect them or who may even abuse them.

Sexuality is an integral part of who we are, what we believe, what we feel, and how we respond to others. Parents have a strong influence on the sexuality of their children. Silence may even speak louder than words.

What to Do

i. Ensure that yourchild understands his/her sexuality.

ii. Do some activities that is common to the child sexualithy

iii. Celebrate your child sexuality

iv. Don't show favouritism according to sexuality

Technology

The term "Technology" is wide and everyone has their own way of understanding the meaning of technology. We use technology to accomplish various tasks in our daily lives. In brief, we can describe technology as products, processes or organizations. We use technology to extend our abilities, and we apply technology in almost everything we do in our lives, we use it at work, to extract materials, for communication, transportation, learning, manufacturing, securing data, scaling businesses and so much more.

When technology is well applied, it can benefit humans, but if it is wrongly applied, it can cause harm to human beings. For example, the smart phone is used for rapid communication between family members who are many miles away from each other. At the same time it can be used for cyber bullying by persons with evil intent.

Many businesses are using technology to stay competitive. They create new products and services using improved technology, and they also use modern technology to deliver those products and services to their customers on time.

Technology and the part it plays in the modern family, is advancing in ways that have accelerated year on year. As technology surrounds us in every aspect of our lives, ignoring it will only result in families being left behind and failing to place the correct importance on technology and its new found role in family life can result in disastrous consequences.

Technology has made our world a fascinating place to live. Access to the abundance of information at our fingertips creates more and new challenges to be considered. Every subject topic or interest can be found at the click of a button.

What to Do

i. To be effective and achieve the best from technology in the family a decision to understand technology, use technology, embrace technology will stand you in a good position to train, develop and guide your family in today's technological age.

ii. Welcome technology and keep up to date as circumstances allow.

iii. Use technology and discuss it in the family

iv. Be aware and informed on technology.

v. Accept responsibility to manage technology. Parent should monitor use of technology such as smart phones, I pods and computers.

Unity

Unity is vital in the family life and has come under attack from the very beginning of the establishment of the family as we know and understand it. If we recognise there is a family in heaven which is united and we are from and connected to it as our heavenly parentage we will see that we have great role models to look to. Mankind is a product of a heavenly union and agreement came into being because of love. So when we talk about unity in a family we can't ignore love, because love is essential in unity.

How we are raised and the connections to our family serve to establish many things about us. Parents play a very large part in forming and shaping our unity and identity in the home and family.

Unity in the family home can sometimes be overlooked, when we allow selfishness and self-centred living to dominate our decisions and choices in life. So a great enemy to unity is selfishness as we begin to move from us, to I and me. Unity costs! The price is usually to sacrifice oneself for the purpose of establishing and maintaining family unity. So in the family there must be a willingness to make sacrifices to maintain peace, harmony and oneness. As we know and is commonly said "unity is strength ".The individuals are the building blocks. Unity must start with decisions to be united and a determination to be united and ongoing choices to be united.

What to Do

i. Establish relevant family rules.

ii. Spend special family time together

iii. Have regular family meetings to reinforce the rules and hear the heartbeat of each family member

iv. Have morning devotion together

v. Ensure every member of the family is given respect.

vi. Celebrate each other's achievements, birthdays and anniversaries.

vii. Recognise the needs of each other and provide support. Where there is special learning needs ensure the whole family is engaged.

viii. Avoid conflicts: resolve problems through solution building and family meetings.

Values

When we live our best life and our most authentic life, it is usually lived from our values. Our values are an important part of the decision process and really define who we are as people. It is important because choices reflect one's values.

Values should be introduced from the onset of relations as it will aid the other person to become conscious of one's position on various matters. Values determine character and behaviour so questions around values would guide persons to vision and the kind of strategies and action to be taken. The core values are the main values which determine a person's character and choices.

Your values are the things that you believe are important in the way you live and work. When the things that you do and the way you behave match your values, life is usually good – you're satisfied and content. But when these don't align with your behaviour there is dissatisfaction. Values should determine your priorities, and, deep down, they're probably the measures you use to tell if your life is turning out the way you want to live it.

Values exist, whether you recognize them or not. Life can be much easier when you acknowledge your values – and when you make plans and decisions that honour them. In these types of situations, understanding your values can really help. When you know your own values, you can use them to make decisions about how to live your life, and you can answer questions like these:

- What job should I pursue?
- Should I accept this promotion?
- Should I start my own business?
- Should I compromise, or be firm with my position?
- Should I follow tradition, or travel down a new path?

So, take the time to understand the real priorities in your life, and you'll be able to determine the best direction for you and your life goals! Values are usually fairly stable, yet they don't have strict limits or boundaries. As you move through life, your values may change. For example, when you start your career, success might be measured by money and status might be a top priority. But after you have a family, work-life balance may be what you value more.

If you value family, but you have to work 70-hour weeks in your job, will you feel internal stress and conflict? And if you don't value competition, and you work in a highly competitive sales environment, are you likely to be satisfied with your job?

What to Do

Identify five main core values which determine the life of your family:

i. Are they in conflict with your personal values?
ii. How are you honouring this in your life?
iii. What are your primary principles?

Wisdom

Wisdom is the ability to discern inner qualities and relationships, which is having insight, good sense and good judgment.

The wisdom in the world is different from Godly wisdom. In the Old Testament the Hebrew for word for wisdom is sakal which means to be circumspect. Our intelligent God tells us where to get it: The fear of the LORD is the beginning of wisdom; all who follow his precepts have good understanding.

According to the Word of God the earthly wisdom is really no wisdom at all because "the wisdom of this world is folly with God" (1 Cor. 3:19). True wisdom is found in obedience to God, fearing Him and His Word, in the Word of God the Bible and by praying or asking for it.

God wants us to have knowledge of Him and what He expects of us. In order to obey Him, we must have knowledge of the commands. But as equally important as having knowledge is having wisdom. Knowing facts about God and the Bible is not all there is to wisdom. Wisdom is a gift from God. James 1:5 states, "If any of you lacks wisdom, you should ask God, who gives generously to all without finding fault, and it will be given to you." God blesses us with wisdom in order for us to glorify Him and use the knowledge we have of Him.

What to Do

1. Establish Godly wisdom being guided by the word.
2. Help your child to know that knowledge is having information but wisdom being able to apply the knowledge
3. Husband and wife should discuss the importance of wisdom
4. Children should be encouraged to ask God for wisdom James 1:5
5. As a family discuss Psalm 37:30

X RelaX and Let Go

Letting go of family members when they seek to be independent can be very difficult. Just step back so that they can go forward. This can be especially challenging when we are raising children in single parent households. Too often, we want to live our unfulfilled dreams through them rather than allowing them to have their own aspirations. Our children's achievements often give us a sense of personal achievement and purpose. To avoid this, we need to continue to fulfill our own ambitions for ourselves. Our personal and professional development should not stop because we are parents. We should make time and create opportunities to grow alongside our children by studying in formal contexts and at home. By nurturing our own growth, we will find strength when our children become teenagers and begin to form other close relationships and assert their independence. Once we have maintained a strong sense of self, when they are ready to leave home, we will be able to celebrate and help them to make the transition, even though it may be painful to experience them leaving.

What to do

i. Plan for your personal and professional development. For example, if you want to take a degree, once your child is older, research where and what you could study well in advance.

ii. On a regular basis arrange for a reliable, experienced and trustworthy person to look after your child so you can have personal time alone with your partner or with friends. Ensure that you explain all arrangements fully to your child.

iii. Try to be a member of at least one group and become actively involved.

iv. Regularly browse the personal development section of your local bookshop for relevant topics. Use the internet as a source of information.

v. Develop close relationships with at least one group of friends, who will help you grow and develop. Spend time with them at least once a month.

vi. Develop your hobbies and interests and share them with your child. Explore career guidance and coaching if you are finding it difficult to decide on a career or to get motivated.

vii. Seek counselling if you know that unresolved issues are preventing you from moving forward.

Y as in Boundary

In family life there are stages and seasons; so a couple who have recently married will not relate to each other in the same as a seasoned couple. They need to love and appreciate each other in every season even when circumstances have changed.

Likewise, it is so important to ensure that each developmental stage in our children's lives is acknowledged, worked through appropriately and celebrated. This is known as the rite of passage. Our children deserve the right to make a safe transition from one stage to the next.

Before we know it, they are out of nappies and leaving home to meet the challenges in the world. We must do our best to prepare them for the journey ahead.

We must establish age appropriate rules and responsibilities to take our children to their next level of physical, spiritual, emotional and intellectual development. Remember, it is our children's right to be given responsibilities.

What to Do

i. Family members should always communicate respectfully with each other

ii. Spouses should work hard to maintain marital integrity and intimacy.

iii. Parents should ensure that they use age appropriate language and behaviour with their child.

iv. Make sure you are fair when setting rules by:
- knowing the developmental stages and work within their remit
- ensuring that safety and non-negotiable issues are enforced with explanations; and
- treating each child according to their stage of development.

v. With a younger child, be sure to constantly reinforce what you expect and need them to do.

vi. Be willing to negotiate certain rules and activities with an older child. Give appropriate responsibilities to develop their skills further, for example, getting home on time and preparing the table for family dinner

vii. Honour what was negotiated, financial and otherwise even If your child does something else that upsets you. If this is the case discuss, the behaviour you are concerned about and work on an appropriate consequence for that unacceptable behaviour.

viii. Celebrate the journey into adolescence for boys and girls. The beginning of menstruation for girls needs to be seen as positive. For example mother and daughter, could go away for the week-end

Zero Tolerance for Abuse

No abuse – sexual or otherwise - should be tolerated within the family. Girls and women should understand that abuse must never be tolerated. They themselves should never be abusers. Likewise, men and boys, who are physically stronger than women and girls, should be trained to be protective of the females.

Sexual and physical abuse can happen under our noses. We need to zoom right in on what our children are saying and doing. Reluctance to visit someone could be more significant than we think. The abuser could be the person we trusted most to look after our children. Let us be very aware and vigilant.

Sometimes we emotionally abuse our children from constantly shouting and criticising or neglecting them in favour of our own pursuits and interests. Sometimes we smack our children believing it to be for their own good, since that was our own childhood experience, hence not realising the damage and hurt we are causing.

It is important that we are able to recognise the symptoms of physical and emotional abuse. As the symptoms often overlap with each other and other medical conditions, we must always check with our doctor to be sure. If there is abuse, we must talk sensitively with our children and seek professional support.

There is contact information for organisations that may be able to help at the back of this book.

What to Do

How to recognise Mental Abuse and Emotional Abuse

There are likely to be signs of:
i. depression, emotional withdrawal or social isolation
ii. sleep disorders, excessive anxiety, speech disorders for example, stammering
iii. self-mutilating behaviours, extremely low self-esteem, addictions to drugs such as alcohol and suicidal tendencies
iv. attention-seeking behaviours, telling lies, tantrums past the age when this is part of normal development
v. inability to have fun , inability to play and indiscriminate displays of affection. , , , , ,

How to recognise Sexual abuse

There are likely to be signs of:
i. bruises or scratches inconsistent with accidental injury,
ii. difficulty in walking or sitting, pain or itching in the genital area, torn, stained or bloody underclothes,
iii. bedwetting, sleep disturbances, loss of appetite,
iv. hints of sexual activity through words, play,

        drawing etc., use of sexually explicit language
- v. poor self-esteem, withdrawal or isolating self from other children

How to recognise Physical abuse

There are likely to be signs of:

- i. facial bruising, hand or finger marks or pressure bruising,
- ii. bite marks, burns (particularly cigarette burns), scalds, unexpected fractures, lacerations or abrasions,
- iii. shying away from physical contact, withdrawn or aggressive behaviour or inexplicable changes in behaviour.

Karlene Rickard is a childcare expert who has overcome paralysis in order to write an acclaimed parent's guide to raising happy, well-adjusted children.

Karlene began her career as a science teacher and later got involved in community work and counselling. She has worked extensively as a parent facilitator, trainer and counsellor in the UK, USA, Jamaica, Grenada and Trinidad for over 15 years. Her powerful 'Empowerment for Parents' parenting programme is credited with changing lives and creating happier families.

She co-founded KJ Academy, a supplementary school in Leyton, East London, and a nursery/infant school in Jamaica where she worked holistically with families to develop their confidence and self-worth.

Karlene is determined to do all she can to have a positive and lasting impact on society through empowering families to raise their children as happy, successful adults who will build healthy communities.

She created 'Empowerment for Parents' programme and published the A to Z of parenting, a simple, easy-to-digest guide. Unlike other childcare manuals, the guide places equal emphasis on the wellbeing of both parent and child, recognising that physically and emotionally stressed adults are unlikely to be great parents, in spite of their best intentions.

Karlene developed a family primary school in Jamaica; she was one of the pioneer facilitators in the UK of the innovative programme Strengthening Families, Strengthening Communities, and she presented the programme in the USA at a fatherhood conference 2001.

Karlene's book, The A to Z of Parenting, deals with parents giving clear and honest feedback to their children and dealing with behavioural challenges. It highlights the value of spending quality time with children, outlines ways to educate them in the early years and focuses on the critical life skills that will carry them through to successful adulthood.

Karlene was awarded the Millennium award in 1999 for developing a parenting programme for African Caribbean families.

Karlene's autobiography, "He Speaks" has been widely read and has spread her message that positive relationship, genuine love and being attuned to the voice of voice of God is essential to build well-balanced adults. She has achieved all of this despite the challenge of living with Multiple Sclerosis.

Mary Crowley OBE
Chair, International Federation for Parenting Education

www.ingramcontent.com/pod-product-compliance
Lightning Source LLC
Chambersburg PA
CBHW071035080526
44587CB00015B/2624